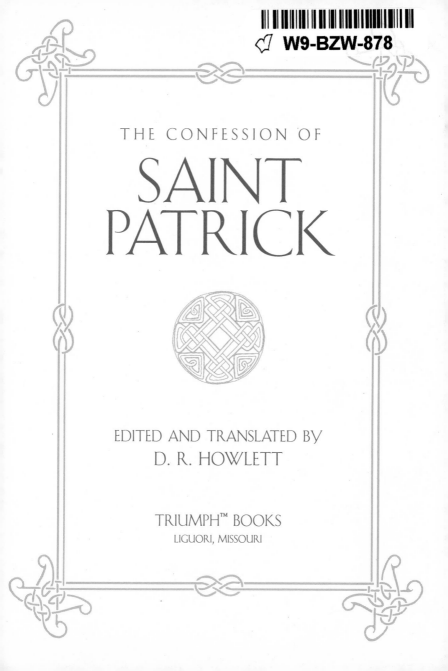

THE CONFESSION OF

SAINT PATRICK

EDITED AND TRANSLATED BY
D. R. HOWLETT

TRIUMPH™ BOOKS
LIGUORI, MISSOURI

Published by Triumph™ Books
Liguori, Missouri
An Imprint of Liguori Publications

The translation of the *Confessio* is taken from *The Book of Letters of Saint Patrick the Bishop* (Dublin, 1994), and is kindly reproduced with the permission of Four Courts Press, Kill Lane, Blackrock, Dublin, Ireland.

Library of Congress Cataloging-in-Publication Data

Patrick, Saint, 373?-463?
    [Confessio. English]
    The confession of Saint Patrick / edited and translated by D. R. Howlett.
        p. cm.
    Includes bibliographical references.
    ISBN 0-89243-881-9
    1. Patrick, Saint, 373?-463? 2. Christian saints—Ireland—Biography.   I. Howlett, D. R. (David R.)   II. Title.
    BR1720.P26A313 1996
    270.2'092–dc20
    [B]   95-38483
                                                             CIP

Printed in the United States of America

9 8 7 6 5 4 3

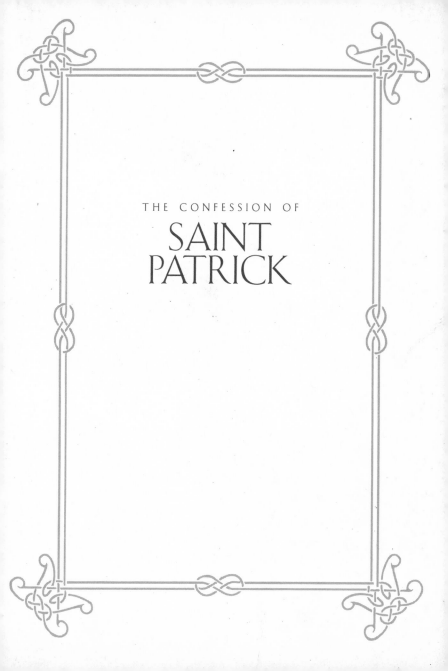

THE CONFESSION OF

SAINT PATRICK

CONTENTS

PATRICK'S CONFESSION: AN INTRODUCTION

The fourth year of [king] Laeghaire, Saint Patrick came to this Island and proceeded to baptize and bless Irish men, women, sons, and daughters except a few who did not consent to receive faith or be baptized by him, as his *Life* relates.

— *The Annals of the Four Masters*

To understand the real Saint Patrick necessitates a literary archaeological excavation that can cut through the layers of accumulated legend, myth, and mystification. The first layer is rather easy to clear up. We can brush away the rubble of popular culture (the parades, green beer, and dinners of cabbage and corned beef consumed to the tremulous renditions of "Danny Boy") as well as the legends (that the saint drove the snakes from Ireland) and the pious tales (his use of the shamrock to explain the mystery of the Trinity). This excavation is not done to debunk or to suggest that such accretions are without cultural or religious or national value; it is only to say that there is a distinction to be made between the bedrock of historical fact and the aura that grows up around the fact.

The second layer demands more historical skills than this nonexpert possesses. It revolves around a very simple but difficult question: What is the historical value of the documents about Saint Patrick (hagiographical *Lives, Annals,* and the *Life*) that emerged in the seventh century and continued to be produced through the medieval period? Recent Patrician scholars seem to be unanimous in their judgment: There may be faint echoes of facts in these later productions, but, in essence, they are not helpful at all in learning about the real Patrick.

If the later legends, annals, and lives do not help historically, they are not without interest; indeed, many scholars study these later sources not for what they tell us of Saint Patrick but for what they reveal about the times in which they were written. One use to which these stories of Saint Patrick were put was to link his name with specific places in order to give the places a special resonance through connection with the saint.

That leaves us then at the bedrock foundation of our excavation: two documents that come from the pen of the saint. One of these documents is a letter to the soldiers of a certain Coroticus bitterly protesting British slave trading of captured Christians whom Patrick himself had received into the Church. The other, luckily for us, is an autobiographical reflection (though it is not technically an autobiography in our sense of the term) entitled the *Confessio*. It is from that latter document that we detect almost everything we know of the saint.

What, in fact, do we know of Saint Patrick from the *Confessio?*

He was born in the western part of

Roman Britain to a Christian family; his father, a *decurio* (town council member), was a deacon, and his grandfather had been a priest. Around the age of sixteen he was taken by Irish raiders and placed in slavery as a herdsman somewhere in Ireland. It was in this period of solitude that he developed his habits of prayer. After six years of servitude he was either freed or escaped, and, after a series of adventures vaguely described by Patrick himself, he returned to his home. It was there that he underwent some training in the Latin Bible and some initiation into the clerical life.

Patrick was not the first bishop in Ireland. Pope Celestine had sent Bishop Palladius to Ireland to "minister to the Irish who believe in Christ" in 431. When Patrick went to Ireland in the 430s, he settled in the North,

probably near Armagh (probably because the greatest of the Irish kings
lived there), and let his mission radiate
out from that area. I say "probably near
Armagh" because some scholars think
that the later chroniclers may have insisted on that point in order to bolster
Armagh's claim to ecclesiastical pri-
macy based on an association with the
saint. Evidently, he spent little or no
time among the already Christianized
in the southeast portion of the island.
Indeed, one could argue that the most
singular thing about Patrick's sojourn
in Ireland was his determination to
convert the pagan population and not
satisfy himself with ministering to those
who, like the flock of Palladius, "already believed in Christ." That may not
seem exceptional to us today, but Patrick's mission to the pagan population
of Ireland is one of the first instances

of a primary evangelization strategy undertaken outside the Roman Empire whose target was a non-Christian population. In a recent book Liam De Paor makes that point with singular force:

His remarkable achievement was to found a new kind of church, one which broke the imperial Roman mould and was both Catholic and barbarian. And he broke the Roman church mould by going among the barbarians. His memory faded after his death but was revived, almost certainly through the accident of the survival of his two writings. That accident was a fitting one, for he was a singular man.

(*Saint Patrick's World,* p. 95)

We do not know the precise character of Patrick's apostolate. He encouraged both men and women to take up the consecrated life, although there is no evidence that he himself was a monk. Patrick's church was an episcopal one; the great period of Celtic monasticism was yet to come. He was a vigorous opponent of paganism and a preacher to all classes. We might imagine his work as a round of evangelizing, preaching, baptizing, and "church planting." As his writings show, he was acutely conscious of his own past life as a slave so that his vehement denunciation of slave-holding in his letter to Coroticus must have reflected his own bitter experiences. Both the letter to Coroticus and his *Confessio* indicate that he spent his own patrimony for the good of the Church. How he managed to build churches and supply the necessities of his mission is not told. The one thing he says, again with great vigor, is that he never profited from the thousands that he brought to the church for baptism. His name is associated with some ancient sites in Ireland like Croagh Patrick (a mountain that is still a pilgrimage site in County Mayo) and towns with names like Down Patrick; but whether they were sites of his missions or merely places that became associated with his cult is almost as uncertain as places in England and even France are associated with his person. Indeed, some scholars think that there may have been more than one Patrick, although this opinion has not received much support. In County Donegal the arduous pilgrimage site of Lough Derg is associated with his name, but its origins can only be traced to the medieval period.

Patrick died circa 461, and his feast

day is March 17. He is honored with the title of both bishop and apostle of Ireland. Although he did not single-handedly bring the faith to Ireland, there is no doubt that he easily deserves the title that adorns his reputation to this day.

What can we say about Saint Patrick's spirituality?

We might begin by noting that the title of his work, the *Confessio,* has a double meaning in Christian Latin. Both Saint Augustine's work and that of Patrick bear a title that indicates two things. First, "confession" means an admission of sin, and Patrick sets out that meaning in the opening sentence: "I, Patrick, a sinner." Secondly, however, "confession" also means an act of faith; many of the early creeds were called both professions of faith and confessions of faith.

That dual sense of the word "confession" helps us understand better Patrick's work. Patrick wants to make two things very plain about himself — namely, that he was a sinner and, with the grace of God, he became a true follower of Christ. And, to be sure, it was a grace, for, as Patrick says, God "kept watch over me before I knew Him."

Patrick is, in the famous formulation of William James, a "twice-born" person. Born into a Christian family, he was not much interested in his faith until, during his days of captivity, he turned to God. One notes many "prison" parallels in the history of the saints. Francis of Assisi began a similar process of conversion after his year in the dungeons of Perugia just as Saint John of the Cross would compose, in the fastness of a monastic prison, one of the most sublime mystical poems of the Christian tradition, "The Spiritual Canticle."

The second extraordinary impression the *Confessio* makes on the reader is its deep Trinitarian faith. Patrick was writing in the fifth century. The deep divisions and disputes about the divinity and humanity of Christ and the divinity of the Holy Spirit had been the subject of intense debate, and some of the great conciliar documents (Constantinople, Ephesus, and Chalcedon) had been issued within his own lifetime. We hear echoes of the creeds in the *Confessio,* but what we hear even more insistently is the living presence of God the Father who watches over Patrick and the glorious Jesus Christ who is hymned throughout the document ("I have known Him from my youth . . ." and the Spirit who writes in hearts not with ink but with presence — the indwelling Spirit). Patrick quotes the Epistle to the Romans more than any other book, and from it he gleans, in the words of the great Patrician scholar R. P. C. Hanson, "a conviction of God's goodness, love, care, and providence towards those who know Him and seek Him and a boundless sense of gratitude for this goodness" (*Saint Patrick,* p. 202).

The third thing I detect in the *Confessio* is Patrick's clear and unwavering sense of his mission: to preach the gospel of Christ to those who lived, as he phrased it in one way or another, in the remote parts of the earth; at the edge of the inhabited world. In his *Confessio* he says that it is necessary to be a "fisher of souls." His audience was, in his words, "this strange people." To his critics who, it would seem, had accused Patrick of self-enrichment, he answers that he sold his own patrimony for the good of the Church; that he taught everyone equally; that he returned unsolicited gifts; that he insisted that of the thousands he had baptized, not one gave him a personal gift. Neither fear of a return to slavery nor a fear of death holds awe for Patrick, for, in the nice phrase of this translator, "I have hurled myself into the hands of all-powerful God who rules as Lord everywhere."

This sense of mission is at the heart of the *Confessio*. As the Irish theologian Noel Dermot O'Donoghue has pointed out in his *Aristocracy of Soul: Saint Patrick of Ireland* (1987), Patrick's work is not a detailed description of his interior development after the manner of Augustine's *Confessions* or

Saint Teresa of Avila's *Mi Vida*. It is a stoutly vigorous defense of the Irish mission and Patrick's legitimate vocation to undertake that mission.

One can only speculate whether Patrick's insistence on his mission to this remote area (well outside the "civilized" world of the Roman Empire) as an urgent task has some eschatological significance. Did he think that when the gospel was preached there, the Lord might come to bring to a close human history? It is hard to say, but his urgency is as clear as his conviction that "We look hopefully for his advent, soon to be." It is impossible, of course, to plumb Patrick's mind fully, but it is not an exaggeration to say that his urgency puts one in mind of the apostle Paul, who urged preaching "in season and out" until the Lord would come again. It is also worth remarking that both Saint Jerome and Saint Augustine note in their writings that the gospel is at last being preached at the edges of the known world. After the sack of Rome in 410, could they not in fact be living in the end time, as evidenced by the gospel's spread?

The Saint Patrick who emerges from the *Confessio* has more to recommend him than the ersatz saint of legend. This is a real person, conscious of his flaws, a recipient of dreams, and possessor of a burning love for Christ and the gospel. Patrick knew the depths of servitude as well as humiliation at the hands of the more sophisticated. He was a lover of the poor and a rescuer of the lost. He was indefatigable in the service of the gospel as he preached to the wild Irish of his day. He is acutely conscious of living outside the pale of the civilized world (even if that world, in his day, was in its final agony). That Patrick wrote in a still-to-be-evangelized territory only adds further interest to his work.

What Patrick did not know was that a century and a half after his work was done, a new generation of Irish missionary monks would not only create a flourishing culture but would send forth missionaries to the continent of Europe and, from places like Iona, keep the torch of learning and culture burning bright. Some of the more adventurous of them would go into self-exile (the greatest of monastic penances) and may have landed in what was later to be called the New World.

From the time I was a child I had a copy of the famous "Breastplate" (lorica) of Saint Patrick; it is a prayer that reads: "Christ with me / Christ before me / Christ behind me / Christ over me / Christ to the right of me / Christ to the left of me / Christ where I lie down / Christ where I sit / Christ where I rise / Christ in the heart of everyone who judges me / Christ in the mouth of everyone who speaks to me / Christ in every eye that sees me / Christ in every ear that hears me." In Irish the prayer is known as the *Faith Fiada* — the "Deer's Cry" used probably as a prayer-charm invoking Christ to keep evil away. It is of great antiquity.

A spectacular prayer! Did Patrick write it? More than likely, if we believe the scholars, Patrick did not compose the prayer, but whoever reads the *Confessio* can well argue that the sentiments of the prayer are not only congruent with but a variation on a base note that runs throughout Patrick's writing: the powerful presence of the Word who created, who became flesh, who dwells among us, and who will return at the end of the days. Patrick's *Confessio* is saturated with the presence of Christ who is present in the world in an almost palpable fashion.

We who read Patrick today cannot shake the legendary Patrick from our imaginations, and there is no reason why we should. However, as we noted at the beginning of this brief meditation, there is something valuable about looking back to the real Patrick as far away from us as he is both in time and in culture. The value is this: Patrick belonged to the same tradition, professed the same faith, preached the same gospel, had the same concern for the poor, and, yes, had the same weaknesses and doubts as we have (or should have) today. In other words, when we come in contact with a person who is separated from us by a millennium and a half, it is edifying to know that somehow we recognize him, his faith, and his sentiments. As many scholars have noted, his two writings are the only evidence we have of what the fifth-century Church looked like outside the borders of the Roman Empire.

To be a Catholic Christian is not only a matter of adhering to a creed. It is, rather, to enter into a story that is both retold in the proclamation of the gospel and reenacted in those rituals we call sacraments. Patrick heard his story from his already Christianized parents; he retold and reenacted that story for those "strange people" who were called the Irish. They, in turn, retold the story in their own land and continue, through their missionary efforts, to tell it not only to themselves but to others around the globe. To read

Patrick's *Confessio,* in short, is to be privy to a part of a long conversation (even though we only catch a snatch of that fifth-century conversation!) that extends down to our own day. A saint, as well as a saint's writings, remind us that we are all part of a people who have more in common through our faith than we do through our background or culture. Beyond its historical value, estimable though it may be, the *Confessio* is also a document that gives witness to the continuity of the Faith. For both reasons we should be grateful.

The Irish have turned Patrick into a symbol of nationalism and native pride as everyone who has ever watched the New York Saint Patrick's Day parade can attest. It is an old tradition. A seventeenth-century English traveler, Thomas Dinely, observed the day in

1681 when "Ye Irish of all stations and conditions wear crosses in their hats, some of pins, some of green ribbons, and the vulgar superstitiously wear shamroges [sic], 3 leaved grass, which they likewise eat, they say, to cause a sweet breath." Long may the custom live; but beyond the custom, let us also honor a man whom we know only through two short documents — documents that exude the spirit of Christ and the missionary bishop inspired by Him. Let Patrick himself have the final word:

Did I come to Ireland without God or according to the flesh? Who compelled me? I am bound by the Spirit not to see any of my kindred. . . . In the end, I am a slave in Christ to a foreign people for the ineffable glory of life everlasting which is in Jesus Christ our Lord.

(*Letter to Coroticus*)

LAWRENCE S. CUNNINGHAM
Professor of Theology and
Chair of the Department
The University of Notre Dame

WORKS CITED

De Paor, Liam. *Saint Patrick's World*. Notre Dame, IN: University of Notre Dame Press, 1993.

Hanson, R.P.C. *Saint Patrick: His Origins and Career*. New York: Oxford University Press, 1968.

McMahon, Sean (ed). *A Book of Irish Quotations*. Springfield, IL: Templegate, 1984.

O'Donoghue, Noel D. *Aristocracy of Soul: Patrick of Ireland Series: The Way of the Christian Mystics*. Wilmington, DE: Glazier, 1987.

TRANSLATOR'S INTRODUCTION

Engagement with the works of Saint Patrick has provided a wonderful form of play, in which three lines of interest have converged: ancestral ties with the *parochia Patricii,* professional association with the Royal Irish Academy's *Dictionary of Medieval Latin from Celtic Sources,* and intense private pleasure in learning to listen to the words of a great saint.

If Patrick was a *homo unius libri* (a man of one book), he had read, marked, learned, and inwardly digested that book. He appropriated not only the words, but the inner meanings and habits of thought he had found in the Latin Bible and internalized them to a remarkable degree, as we shall see both in his quotations from and allusions to Biblical texts and in his structuring of narrative.

The Biblical models for his fivefold division of the *Confession* are the five books of the Pentateuch and their New Testament reflex in the five collections of sayings of Jesus in St. Matthew's Gospel.

Part I corresponds to Genesis, relating Patrick's beginnings and early history, rising to the first great climax in the Apology, where the concern with language may be compared with the account of Babel and Patrick's captivity in Ireland may be compared with Joseph's captivity in Egypt.

Part II corresponds to Exodus, in which the herdsman Patrick escapes from captivity across the sea like the shepherd Moses. His journey of four weeks through the desert may be compared with the Israelites' journey of four decades through the desert, his miraculous feeding with their manna, the provision of fire during his journey with the pillar of fire during the Israelites' journey, his vision of God with Moses's vision of God on Mount Sinai.

Part III corresponds to Leviticus, relating Patrick's dealings with ecclesiastical authorities and his own ecclesiastical status.

Part IV corresponds to Numbers, relating Patrick's account of his conversions, baptisms, confirmations, and ordinations.

Part V corresponds to Deuteronomy, concluding with Patrick's preparation for death.

Patrick's *Epistola* and *Confessio* are dense compositions not only filled with delights for the ears, eyes, and minds of the attentive, but armed with defenses against careless reproduction, incompetent editing, and ignorant reading by the insensitive. Modern scholars, by ignoring the defenses, have missed many of the delights. They have taken at face value Patrick's apparent confessions of ignorance and inelegance, conveying to modern readers a notion that he was an incoherent thinker and inarticulate writer, who could "give an impression of spluttering incoherence"[1] and refer to his own prose as "drivel."[2] The greatest modern editor of the works of Patrick has stated that "the apostle of the Irish was not a *littérateur*"[3] and complained of his "naive rhetoric"[4] and "the vagueness of structure that is so characteristic of his style"[5] and his "constant struggle with the language, and a rather involved way of thinking."[6] Professor Carney has judged him "an inexperienced writer,"[7] and Professor Binchy has described him as the "simple Patrick of the Confessio," a writer of "stumbling barbarous Latin."[8] Bishop Patrick Hanson, one of the most sensible and sensitive students of Patrick's life and work, has stated that

> Patrick could not conduct a sustained argument in Latin. He could not carry through a narrative in a well-ordered way. He had no literary devices, no store of syntactical variations, no reserves of vocabulary, no art at all, in using Latin.[9]

Again:

Patrick's writing is completely devoid of rhetoric. . . . Patrick was incapable of writing for effect. It was all he could do to convey his thoughts to the reader without artifice, and even then he was not always able to do that.[10]

Such scholars have grievously misunderstood and grotesquely misrepresented Patrick by not attending to the lexical connections of his thought. This English translation follows, wherever possible, line for line, mood for mood, voice for voice, word for word the original Latin. It attempts to distinguish *ait, dicit, inquit,* and *locutus est,* and to represent in English the underlying etymological connections of the Latin words, rendering *grauiter* "oppressively" and *grauitudinem* "oppressiveness"; *docere* "to teach," *docui*

"I have taught," *indoctus* "untaught,"
not "unlearned"; *miser* "pitiable," not
"wretched," *miserissime* "most pitiably," *misericordia* "pity," not "mercy';
testatur "he testifies," *testificor* "I bear
testimony," *testimonium* "testimony,"
testis "testifier," not "witness." This may
produce inelegant translation, but it
enables readers of English to note Patrick's repetition of words and ideas.
Only after apprehending the mechan-
ical structure of Patrick's thought and
prose can one begin to hear the tenor
of his explicit statements and the un-
dertones and overtones of his implicit
resonances.

We may take as a model for such
composition the vision of the Prophet
Ezekiel, a captive, like Patrick, in a
foreign land, where he saw *et aspec-
tus earum et opera quasi sit rota in
medio rotae* "both their appearance

and working as if it were a wheel in the middle of a wheel,"[11] like the inclusion of a chiastic sentence within a chiastic paragraph, itself within a chiastic chapter that is part of a chiastic whole. In the account of his sixth vision Patrick describes being within his own body and yet looking down upon someone else praying within him and also hearing the Holy Spirit praying above his interior man. As the Holy Spirit spoke to Patrick, so he speaks to us, through and within and around his narrative, in harmonies that grow more complex, with resonances that reverberate longer, through meanings that become richer and denser every time we return to his texts.

It would be impertinent to try to rescue the works of Patrick from the state into which traditions of misdirected and acrimonious modern scholarship have brought them unless the Apostle of the Irish had provided the means. By listening to him on his own terms we can hear him speak articulately, authoritatively, compellingly, from across fifteen centuries, with a power he believed to be not his own but God's.

NOTES

1. A. B. E. Hood (ed. & transl.), *St Patrick, His Writings and Muirchu's Life,* History from the Sources (London & Chichester, 1978), p. 18.

2. C. H. H. Wright (transl.), The *Writings of St Patrick,* Christian Classics Series VI (3rd ed. enlarged, London, n.d.), p. 49.

3. L. Bieler (ed.), *Libri Epistolarum Sancti Patricii Episcopi, Classica et Mediaevalia* XI (1950), p. 5. Cf. Ibid., p. 28: "The apostle of Ireland was not a man of letters."

4. Idem, *The Life and Legend of St. Patrick, Problems of Modern Scholarship* (Dublin, 1949), p. 73.

5. Idem, *Libri* XI, p. 44.

6. Idem, *Life and Legend,* p. 49.

7. J. Camey, The *Problem of St. Patrick* (Dublin, 1961), p. 94.

8. D. A. Binchy, "Patrick and His Biographers Ancient and Modern," *Studia Hibernica* II (1962), pp. 55, 143.

9. R. P. C. Hanson, *Saint Patrick: His Origins and Career* (Oxford, 1968), p. 163.

10. Idem (transl.), *The Life and Writings of the Historical Saint Patrick* (New York, 1983), p. 36.

ABOUT PATRICK'S TEXT

Professor Ludwig Bieler established the text of Patrick's literary works in a justly famous edition, published with introduction, critical apparatus, and commentary in *Classica et Mediaevalia* XI (1950) and XII (1951),* reprinted as *Libri Epistolarum Sancti Patricii Episcopi* by the Irish Manuscripts Commission (Dublin: Stationery Office, 1952). In 1989 the Royal Irish Academy pub-

*See also L. Bieler (transl.), *The Works of St. Patrick, St. Secundinus Hymn on St. Patrick,* Ancient Christian Writers, The Works of the Fathers in Translation (Westminster, MD & London, 1953).

lished as the third volume in a series ancillary to the *Dictionary of Medieval Latin from Celtic Sources* the *Clavis Patricii I, A Computer-Generated Concordance to the "Libri Epistolarum" of Saint Patrick,* by Kieran Devine with a foreword by Anthony Harvey, based upon Bieler's edition, which is to be reprinted with a bibliography by Dr. Harvey in the same series as *Clavis Patricii II* and *III.* As these excellent works are readily accessible there is no need to reproduce their apparatus, commentary, indices, or bibliography.

The text of Patrick's *Confessio* presented here for the most part follows Bieler's text.

CONFESSION

PART I

I, Patrick, a sinner, very rustic,
and the least of all the faithful,
and very contemptible in the
 estimation of most men,
had as father a certain man called
 Calpornius, a deacon,
son of Potitus, a presbyter,
who was in the town Bannaventa
 Berniae,
for he had a little villa nearby,
where I conceded capture.
In years I was then almost sixteen.

For I was ignorant of the true God,
and I was led to Ireland in captivity
with so many thousands of men
    according to our deserts,
  because we withdrew from God,
and we did not keep watch over His
    precepts,
and we were not obedient to our
    priests,
who kept admonishing our salvation,
and the Lord led down over us the
    wrath of His anger
and dispersed us among many gentiles
    even as far as the furthest part of
    land,
where now my insignificance is seen
    to be among members of a strange
    race.
And there the Lord opened the
    consciousness of my unbelief
so that, perhaps, late, I might
    remember my delicts,

and that I might turn with a whole
   heart to the Lord my God,
Who turned His gaze round on my
   lowliness
and took pity on my adolescence and
   ignorance
and kept watch over me before I knew
   Him
and before I was wise or distinguished
   between good and bad,
and He fortified me
and consoled me as a father
   [consoles] a son.

Whence moreover I cannot be silent,
nor assuredly is it expedient,
about such great benefits
and such great grace,
which the Lord has deigned to supply
   to me
in the land of my captivity,

because this is our reward [lit. "what is
    handed back"]
as after rebuke and acknowledgement
    of God
to exalt and confess His marvels
before every nation
which is under every heaven.
Because there is not another God,
nor ever was before
nor will be after these [times],
besides God the unbegotten Father
without beginning,
from Whom is all beginning,
holding all things,
as we have learned,
and His Son Jesus Christ,
Whom with the Father, to be sure,
we bear witness always to have existed
before the origin of the age,
spiritually begotten with the Father in
    a way that cannot be narrated,
before all beginning,

and through Him have all things been
    made, visible and invisible,
made man,
when death had been utterly con-
    quered, received in the heavens
    with the Father.
And He has given to Him all power
    over every name
of beings celestial
and terrestrial
and of the lower regions,
and every tongue should confess to
    Him
that Jesus Christ is Lord and God,
Whom we believe,
and we look hopefully for His advent,
    soon to be,
the judge of the living and the dead,
Who will give back to each according
    to his own deeds,
and He has poured out abundantly
    among us the Holy Spirit,

a gift and pledge of immortality,
Who makes those believing and
    obeying
that they may be sons of God and
    fellow heirs of Christ,
Whom we confess and adore,
one God in a Trinity of sacred name.

For He Himself has said through the
    prophet,
Call on me in the day of your
    tribulation
and I will free you
and you will magnify me.
And again He affirms,
To reveal and confess, moreover, the
    works of God
is a thing that confers honor.
Nevertheless even if I am imperfect in
    many respects,
I prefer for my brothers and relatives to
    know my quality,

that they may see through to the vow
    of my soul.

I am not ignorant of the testimony of
    my Lord,
Who in the psalm testifies,
You will lose those who speak a lie.
And again He affirms,
The mouth which lies murders the
    soul.
And the same Lord in the Gospel
    affirms
The idle word which men will have
    spoken,
they will give back for it an account on
    the day of judgment.
Whence, moreover, I ought
    vehemently
with fear and trembling to fear this
    sentence
on that day where no man will have

been able to withdraw or hide
    himself,
but we are all entirely bound to give
    back an account,
even of the least sins,
before the tribunal of the Lord Christ.

On which account formerly I thought
    about writing,
but even until now I hesitated,
for I feared lest I should fall onto the
    tongue of men,
because I did not learn just as the
    others also,
who most excellently, consequently,
    drank in laws and sacred letters,
both in equal measure,
and never changed their styles of
    speech from infancy,
but rather added always toward
    perfection.

For our speech and spoken language
    was translated into a strange
    tongue,
as it can easily be proved from the
    savor of my writing
how I was instructed and brought out
    from an uncultivated state in styles
    of speech,
because it affirms Through the tongue
    will the wise man be recognized,
also consciousness and knowledge
    and teaching of the truth.
But with respect to the truth what does
    an excuse profit,
particularly with obstinacy,
since now in my old age I seek
what in my youth I did not establish,
because my sins stood in the way that
    I should confirm
what I had read through before?
But who believes me even if I shall
    have said what I mentioned before?

As an adolescent, more precisely, as an
   almost wordless boy,
I conceded capture
before I knew what I ought to seek
or what to avoid.
Whence therefore today I blush for
   shame
and vehemently thoroughly fear
to strip naked my unlearnedness,
because I cannot unfold in speech to
   those learned in conciseness
as, however, my spirit and mind longs,
and the emotion of my consciousness
   suggests.
But if, consequently, it had been given
   to me just as also to others,
even so I would not be silent on
   account of what should be handed
   back [from me to God].
And if by chance it seems to certain
   men that I put myself forward in this,

with my lack of knowledge and my
   rather slow tongue,
but even so it is, however, written
Stammering tongues will swiftly learn
   to speak peace.
How much more ought we to seek, we
   who are, he affirms,
The letter of Christ for salvation as far
   as the furthest part of land,
and if not learned, yet valid and very
   vigorous,
written in your hearts
not with ink but by the Spirit of the
   living God,
and again the Spirit testifies
even rustic work created by the Most
   High.
Whence I, the extreme rustic,
a refugee, untaught, doubtless,
who do not know how to look forward
   into the future,

but that I do know most certainly, that
   indeed before I was humbled
I was like a stone that lies in deep mud,
and He Who is powerful came
and in His pity He raised me up
and assuredly to be sure lifted me
   upward
and placed me on the highest wall
and therefore I ought forcefully to
   shout out
for something that should be handed
   back to the Lord also
for His benefits so great here and for
   eternity,
which [benefits] the mind of men
   cannot estimate.
Whence, moreover, be astonished,
   consequently,
you great and small who fear God,
and you, sirs [lords], clever
   rhetoricians,
hear therefore and examine

who roused me up, a fool, from the
   midst of those
who seem to be wise and learned by
   experience in law
and powerful in speech and in
   everything
and inspired me, assuredly, beyond
   the others of this execrable world
if I should be such — if only moreover
   [I were] —
that with fear and reverence
and without complaint I should
   proceed faithfully to that gentile
   people
to which the charity of Christ translated
   me
and granted me during my life, if I will
   have been worthy,
that at last with humility and truthfully
   I might serve them.
According to the measure, consequently,

of the faith of the Trinity it is fitting
   to distinguish,
without blame of danger [by hypallage
   "without danger of blame," i.e.,
   "without fear of criticism"]
to make known the gift of God
and [His] eternal consolation,
without fear
in faithworthy fashion to expound
   everywhere the name of God,
in order even after my death to leave
   behind a legacy to my brothers and
   sons
whom I have baptized in the Lord, so
   many thousands of men.

And I was not worthy nor such
that the Lord should allow this to His
   little servant,
after troubles and such great burdens,
after captivity,

after many years among that gentile
    people,
that He should grant such great grace
    to me,
which I never at any time in my youth
    hoped for nor thought about.

PART II

But after I had come to Ireland,
I was consequently pasturing domestic
    animals daily,
and often in the day I was praying.
More and more the love of God and
    fear of Him was approaching,
and faith was being increased, and the
    Spirit was being stirred up,
so that in a single day up to a hundred
    prayers,
and in a night nearly the same,

even as I was staying in forests and on
the mountain,
and before dawn I was roused up to
prayer,
through snow, through frost, through
rain,
and I was feeling nothing bad,
nor was there any sloth in me,
as I see now, because the Spirit was
being fervent in me then,
and there, to be sure, on a certain night
in a dream
I heard a voice saying to me,
"It is well that you are fasting, bound
soon to go to your fatherland."
And again after a very little time
I heard the answer saying to me,
"Look, your ship is ready."
And it was not near,
but perhaps two hundred miles [lit. "it
had two hundred thousand double
paces"],

and I had never been there,
nor did I have any single acquaintance
   among men there,
and then later I turned to flight,
and I abandoned the man with whom I
   had been for six years,
and I came in the power of God,
Who was directing my way toward the
   good,
and I was fearing nothing until I came
   through to that ship,
and on that day on which I came
   through the ship set out from its
   own place,
and I spoke as I had the wherewithal
   to ship with them,
and the captain, it displeased him,
and he responded sharply with
   indignation,
"By no means will you seek to go with
   us."

And when I heard these things I
   separated myself from them,
so that I would come to the little hut
   where I was staying,
and on the journey I began to pray,
and before I could bring the prayer to
   the highest perfection
I heard one of them,
and he was shouting out vigorously
   after me,
"Come soon, because these men are
   calling you,"
and immediately I returned to them,
and they began to say to me,
"Come, because we are receiving you
   on faith,
make friendship with us in whatever
   way you will have wished,"
and on that day, to be sure, I refused to
   suck their nipples
on account of the fear of God,

but nevertheless I hoped to come by
   them to the faith of Jesus Christ,
as they were gentiles,
and because of this I got my way with
   them,
and we shipped at once.

And after a three-day period we
   reached land,
and for twenty-eight days we made a
   journey through the desert,
and food was not forthcoming for
   them,
and hunger prevailed over them,
and on the next day the captain began
   to say to me,
"What is it, Christian?
You say your God is great and all-
   powerful.
Why therefore can you not pray for us,
because we are imperilled by hunger,

for it is not likely that we may ever see
    any man."

But I said confidently to them,
"Be turned in faith with a whole heart
    to the Lord my God,
because nothing is impossible to Him,
so that today He may dispatch food to
    you until you should be satisfied on
    your way,
as there was abundance everywhere
    for Him."

And with God helping it was made so.
Look, a flock of pigs appeared in the
    way before our eyes,
and they killed many of them,
and there they remained two nights
    and were well fed,
and they were refilled with their flesh,
because many of them fainted away,

and were left behind half-alive along
the way,
and after this they gave the highest
thanks to God,
and I was made honorable in their
eyes,
and from this day they had food
abundantly;
they even discovered [lit. "came upon"]
forest honey,
and they offered a part to me,
and one of them said, "It is a [pagan]
sacrifice."
Thanks be to God,
I tasted nothing from it.

But on the same night I was sleeping,
and Satan tried me vigorously,
which I shall be mindful of as long as I
will have been in this body,
and he fell over me like a huge rock,

and none of my members having any
    prevailing power.
But whence came to me in my ignorant
    spirit that I should call Elias?
And amidst these things I saw the sun
    rise into the heaven,
and while I was calling "Elia, Elia" with
    all my powers,
look, the splendor of His sun [ἥλιος]
    fell down over me,
and immediately shook off from me all
    oppressiveness,
and I believe that I was come to the aid
    of by Christ my Lord,
and His Spirit was already then
    shouting for me,
and I hope that it will be so on the day
    of my pressing need,
as He affirms in the Gospel,
On that day,
the Lord testifies, You will not be you
    who speak

but the Spirit of your Father Who
    speaks in you.

And again after many years farther I
    conceded capture.
Consequently on that first night I
    remained with them
I heard moreover a divine answer
    saying to me,
"For two months you will be with
    them,"
which was made so.
On that sixtieth night
the Lord freed me from their hands.
He even foresaw for us on the journey
    food
and fire and dryness daily,
until on the tenth day we came through
    to men.
As I have made known above,
we made a journey through the desert
    twenty and eight days,

and on that night on which we came
through to men we had in truth
nothing of food.

And again after a few years in the
Britains I was
with my parents,
who received me as a son,
and in faith requested me
whether now I, after such great
tribulations which I bore,
I should not ever depart from them.
And there to be sure I saw in a vision
of the night a man coming as if from
Ireland,
whose name [was] Victoricius,
with innumerable epistles,
and he gave me one of them,
and I read the beginning of the epistle
containing "the Voice of the Irish,"
and while I was reciting the beginning
of the epistle

I kept imagining bearing at that very
   moment the voice of those very men
who were beside the Forest of Foclut,
which is near the Western Sea [lit. "the
   sea of the setting (*sc.* of the sun)"],
and thus they shouted out as if from
   one mouth,
"We request you, holy boy,
that you come and walk farther among
   us."
And I was especially stabbed at heart,
and I could not read further.
And thus I have learned by experience,
thanks be to God,
that after very many years the Lord has
   supplied them
according to their clamor.
And on another [or "the second"] night,
   I do not know, God knows,
whether within me or beside me,
in most learned words I heard those
   whom

I could not yet understand,
except that at the very end of the
    prayer one spoke out thus:
"He Who has given His own soul for
    you
He it is Who speaks in you,"
and thus I was awakened rejoicing.
And again I saw Him praying within
    myself,
and I was as if inside my body,
and I heard over me, this is, over the
    interior man,
and there He was praying vigorously
    with groans,
and amidst these things I was stupefied
    and I kept marvelling and thinking
Who He might be Who was praying in
    me,
but at the very end of the prayer thus
    He spoke out that He might be the
    Spirit.
And thus I have learned by experience

and recalled to mind, as the apostle
    says,
The Spirit helps the weaknesses of our
    prayer.
For we do not know, as is fitting, what
    we should pray for,
but the Spirit Himself demands for us
    with groans that cannot be narrated
things which cannot be expressed in
    words.
And again, The Lord our advocate
    demands for us.

PART III

And when I was tried by certain of my
    elders who came
and hurled my sins as a charge against
    my toilsome episcopate,
indeed on that day I was vigorously
    pushed back,
so that I should fall here and for
    eternity,
but the Lord spared a sojourner and
    exile
on account of His own kindly name,

and especially came to my support in
this trampling down,
so that in collapse and in shame I did
not come out badly.
I pray God that it not be reckoned to
them as sin.
After thirty years they discovered
[lit. "came upon," "invented"] an
occasion against me,
a word which I had confessed before I
was a deacon.
On account of anxiety in a mournful
mind I made known to my most
intimate friend
what I had done in my boyhood on
one day,
more precisely in one hour,
because I had not yet prevailing power.
I do not know, God knows
if I then had fifteen years,
and I did not believe the living God,
nor [had I believed] from my infancy,

but I remained in death and in unbelief
until the time I was especially
    castigated,
and in truth I was humiliated
by hunger and nakedness, even daily.

On the other hand I did not proceed to
    Ireland with willing consent
until the time I nearly fainted away.
But this was rather well for me,
who have because of this been freed
    from a fault by the Lord,
and He has fitted me so that today I
    may be
what was once far away from me,
that I may have the care
or rather be occupied with the
    salvation of others,
when moreover at that time I was not
    thinking even about myself.
So then on that day on which I was
    reproved

by those called to mind, the abovesaid,
on that night I saw in a vision of the
   night
what had been written against my face
   without honor,
and amidst these things I heard the
   divine answer saying to me,
"We have seen badly [i.e., "with disap-
   proval"] the face of the man marked
   out with his name stripped naked,"
and He did not say forth, "You have
   seen badly,"
but "We have seen badly,"
as if He had joined me to Himself,
just as He has said, "He who touches
   you
[is] as he who touches the pupil of
   my eye."

Because of that I give thanks to Him
Who has strengthened me in all things,
so that He did not impede me from

setting out on the journey which I
  had decided on,
and also from my task which I had
  learned from Christ my Lord,
but rather from Him I sensed within
  myself a not insignificant power,
and my faith was approved before God
  and men.

Whence moreover I say boldly
my conscience does not reprehend me
here and for the future.
I have with God as witness
that I have not lied
in the speeches which I have referred
  to you.

But I grieve the more for my most
  intimate friend,
because we deserved to hear such an
  answer from this man,
to whom I entrusted even my soul.

And I have discovered from certain
   brothers
before that defense,
because I was not present,
nor was I in the Britains,
nor did it arise from me,
that he also in my absence would
   importune for me.
He himself had even said to me from
   his own mouth,
"Look, you are to be given over to the
   grade of the episcopate,"
which I was not worthy of.
But whence did it come to him
   afterwards
that in the sight of all, good and bad,
he should dishonor me even publicly
over something he had conceded
   before happy and with willing
   consent,
and the Lord, Who is greater than all.

I say enough.
But nevertheless I ought not to hide
     the gift of God,
which has been granted to us in the
     land of my captivity,
because then I vigorously sought Him,
and there I found Him,
and He kept me from all iniquities, so
     I believe,
on account of His indwelling Spirit,
Who has worked up to this day in me.

Boldly again,
But, God knows, if a man had spoken
     this out to me,
perhaps I would have been silent
     about the charity of Christ.

Whence therefore I give unwearied
     thanks to my God,
Who has kept me faithful on the day of
     my trial,

so that today I may confidently offer
    sacrifice to Him,
my soul as a living host to Christ my
    Lord,
Who has kept me from all my straits,
so that I also may say, "Who am I, Lord,
or what is my calling,"
[You] Who have appeared to me with
    such divinity,
so that today among gentiles
I may constantly exalt
and magnify Your name
in whatever place I shall have been
and not only in favorable circum-
    stances,
but also in pressing needs,
so that whatever will have happened
    to me,
either good or bad,
I ought to undertake equally,
and always to give thanks to God,
Who has shown to me

that I should believe Him indubitable
   without end,
and He Who will have heard me,
so that I unknowing and in the final
   days
may dare to approach this work so
   pious and so wondrous,
so that I to some degree may imitate
   those
whom the Lord long before now had
   said beforehand
as going to herald His own Gospel,
as a testimonial to all the gentiles
   before the end of the world,
which we therefore have seen so, and
   so it has been fulfilled.
Look, we are testifiers that the Gospel
   has been proclaimed
as far as where there is no man beyond.
It is, moreover, longwinded to relate
   my labor by single examples, or in
   parts.

Briefly I shall say how the most pious
   God has often freed from slavery
and from twelve perils in which my
   soul was imperilled,
besides many treacheries
and things which I am not able to
   express in words.
I shall not make an injustice for those
   reading,
but I have God as authority,
Who knows all things even before they
   may be done,
that me, a poor little pupil,
an ordinary person [His] divine answer
   would frequently admonish.

Whence [came] to me this wisdom,
which was not in me,
who knew neither the number of days,
nor did I have any wisdom about God?
Whence [came] to me afterward the gift
   so great, so salutary,

to acknowledge or to love God dearly,
but that I would lose fatherland and
    parents?

And many gifts kept being offered to
    me with weeping and tears,
and I offended those [who gave them],
and also against [my] wish a certain
    number of my elders,
but with God acting as captain in
    no way did I agree with them nor
    acquiesce,
not by my grace but God Who
    conquers in me,
and stood firm against them all,
as I had come to Irish gentiles to
    proclaim the Gospel,
and to endure indignities from
    unbelievers,
so that I might hear shame of my exile,
and many persecutions up to the point
    of chains,

and so that I might give up my freeborn
    status for the advantage of others,
and if I will have been worthy I am
    quick to respond,
so that [I might give up] even my soul,
unhesitatingly and most willingly for
    His name.

PART IV

And there I prefer to spend it up to the
    point of death,
if the Lord should concede to me,
because I am especially a debtor [lit.
    "ower"] to God,
Who has granted to me such great
    grace,
that many people through me should
    be reborn to God,
and afterwards brought to the highest
    perfection,

and that clerics everywhere should be
   ordained for them,

for a folk coming recently to belief,

whom the Lord has taken up from the
   most remote parts of land,

just as formerly He had promised
   through His own prophets:

To you gentiles will come from the
   most remote parts of land, and they
   will say,

Our fathers established idols as false
   things,

and there is no advantage in them.

And again: I have placed you as a light
   among the gentiles,

so that you may be for salvation as far
   as the most remote part of land,

and there I wish to wait hopefully for
   the promise of Him,

Who indeed never deceives.

Just as He guaranteed in the Gospel,

They will come from the rising and the
setting [i.e., from east and west],
and they will lie back with Abraham
and Isaac and Jacob,
just as we believe that those believing
are bound to come from all the
world.
Because of that consequently it is
fitting assuredly to fish well and with
loving care,
just as the Lord admonishes in advance
and teaches, saying,
Come after me and I will make you to
be made fishers of men,
and again He says through the
prophets,
Look, I send fishers and many hunters,
says God, and the other parts.
Whence moreover it was especially
fitting to extend our nets,
so that a plentiful multitude and throng
should be captured for God,

and everywhere there should be clerics
who would baptize,
and exhort a needing and desiring
people,
just as the Lord affirms in the Gospel,
He admonishes and teaches, saying,
Going therefore teach now all the
gentiles,
baptizing them in the name of the
Father and the Son and the Holy
Spirit,
teaching them to observe all things
whatsoever I have commanded to
you,
and look, I am with you all days,
as far as the highest perfection of the
age.
And again He says, Going therefore
into the entire world,
proclaim the Gospel to every creature.
He who will have believed and been
baptized will be saved,

but he who will not have believed will
   be condemned.
And again, Proclaim this Gospel of the
   Realm in the entire world,
for testimony to all gentiles,
and then the end will come.
And similarly the Lord announces
   beforehand through the prophet, He
   affirms,
And it will be in the final days, says the
   Lord,
I will pour out from my Spirit over all
   flesh,
and your sons and your daughters will
   prophesy,
and your youths will see visions,
and your elders will dream dreams,
and assuredly over my slaves
and over my handmaids in those
   days,
I will pour out from my Spirit and
   they will prophesy.

And in Hosea He says, I will call "not
    my folk" "my folk,"
and "not having acquired pity" "having
    acquired pity,"
and there will be in the place where
    "you [are] not my folk" was said,
there they will be called sons of the
    living God.
Whence moreover in Ireland those
    who never had notice of God,
up to now they always worshipped
    nothing except idols and unclean
    things,
how recently a folk of the Lord has
    been made,
and they are named sons of God.
The sons and daughters of the petty
    kings of the Scots
are seen to be monks and virgins of
    Christ,
and there was even one blessed
    Scotswoman, noble from birth,

most beautiful as a grown woman,
whom I baptized,
and after a few days for one cause she
    came to us,
she made known to us that she had re-
    ceived an answer from a messenger
    of God,
and he monished her that she should
    be a virgin of Christ,
and that she should draw near to
    God.
Thanks be to God,
on the sixth day from this she most ex-
    cellently and most eagerly accepted
    that,
because all virgins of God do this even
    so,
not with the willing assent of their
    fathers,
but they even suffer persecutions
and false reproaches from their own
    parents,

and nonetheless their number is
    increased more,
and those who have been born from
    our begetting,
we do not know their number,
besides widows and continent women.
But they also labor most who are
    detained in service;
they bear continually [everything] up
    to the point of terrors and threats,
but the Lord has given grace to many
    of His own handmaids,
for even if they are forbidden, never-
    theless they imitate this conduct
    vigorously.

Whence moreover even if I should
    have wished to lose them,
so that proceeding even to the Britains,
and most willingly I was prepared,
as if to fatherland and parents,
not only that,

but even as far as the Gauls to visit
    brothers,
and that I might see the face of the holy
    men of my Lord.
God knows what I preferred
    especially,
but bound by the Spirit,
Who protests to me if I shall have done
    this,
that He marks me out to be guilty for
    the future,
and I fear to lose the labor which I
    have begun,
and not I,
but Christ the Lord
Who has commanded me
that I should come to be with them for
    the rest of my lifetime,
if the Lord will have wished,
and He will have kept watch over me
    from every bad way,
so that I do not sin before Him.

I hope moreover that I ought [or "was
  bound" to do] this,
but I do not believe in myself,
for as long as I will have been in this
  body of death,
because he is vigorous, he who strives
  daily to subvert me from the faith
and from the chastity of a religion not
  feigned set before [me],
up to the end of my life for Christ my
  Lord.
But the inimical flesh always drags
  toward death,
that is, toward allurements to be dealt
  with illicitly,
and I know in part why I have not lived
  a perfect life,
just as the others also believing,
but I confess to my Lord,
and I do not blush for shame in His
  sight,
as I do not lie,

because I have known Him from my
    youth,
in me the love of God and fear of Him
    has grown,
and up to now, with the Lord favoring,
    I have kept the faith.
Let him who will have wished
    moreover laugh and insult,
I shall not be silent, nor do I hide signs
    and wonders,
which have been shown to me by the
    Lord
many years before they may be made,
as He Who knows all things even
    before the times of the ages.

Whence moreover I ought [or "was
    bound"] to give thanks without
    ceasing to God,
Who has often conceded to my
    unwisdom,
to my carelessness,

even out of place, not on one
[occasion] either,

that He would not grow vehemently
angry with me,

who have been given as a helper,

and I did not acquiesce quickly according to what had been shown to
me,

and just as the Spirit was suggesting
to me,

the Lord has shown pity to me up to
thousands of thousands of times,

because He saw in me that I was
ready,

but that I did not know for myself for
these circumstances,

what I should do about my own
condition,

because many were hindering this
embassy.

They were even talking among
themselves behind my back

and saying, "Why does this man
    dispatch himself in peril
among enemies who do not know
    God?"
Not as from a cause of malice,
but it did not seem wise to them,
just as I myself bear witness,
to be understood on account of my
    rusticity,
and not quickly did I acknowledge the
    grace which was then in me.
Now what I ought [to have done]
    before seems wise to me.

Now therefore I have simply made
    known to my brothers and fellow
    slaves,
who have believed in me on account
    of what I have said beforehand and
    proclaim,
for corroborating and confirming your
    faith.

Would that you also imitate the greater
    things and perform more powerful
    things.
This will be my glory,
because a wise son
is the glory of a father.
You know, God also, how I have
    conducted myself among you
from my youth
in the faith of truth and in sincerity of
    heart.
Even to these gentiles among whom I
    dwell
I have supplied and I will supply faith
    to them [i.e., "I have kept and I will
    keep my word to them"].
God knows I have cheated [lit. "gone
    round"] none of them,
nor do I think, on account of God and
    His Church,
that I would rouse up persecution for
    them and all of us,

nor that the name of the Lord should
    be blasphemed through me,
because it is written, Woe to the man
through whom the name of the Lord is
    blasphemed.
For even if I am unlearned in all things,
nevertheless I have tried to some
    degree to save myself,
even also for Christian brothers
and virgins of Christ and religious
    women,
who kept giving me voluntary little
    gifts,
and they kept hurling some of their
    own ornaments over the altar,
and I kept giving them back again to
    them,
and they kept being scandalized in
    response to me because I kept doing
    this.
But I on account of the hope of
    everlastingness,

so that I would preserve myself
    cautiously in all things on that
    account,
so that they would not on any legal
    charge of unfaithfulness capture me
or the ministry of my slavery,
nor would I give a place even in
    the least degree to unbelievers to
    defame or detract.
Perhaps moreover when I baptized so
    many thousands of men
I would have hoped for even half a
    scruple [i.e., $1/576$ of a unit] from any
    of them.
Tell me, and I will give it back to you.
Or when the Lord ordained clerics
    everywhere
through my littleness and I distributed
    the ministry to them free,
if I asked for even the price even of my
    shoe from any of them,

tell it to my face and I will give more
back to you.
I have spent for you that they might
receive [lit. "capture"] me,
and among you and everywhere I
proceeded in your cause in many
perils,
even as far as remote parts,
where there was no man beyond,
and where no one had ever come
through,
who would baptize
or ordain clerics
or bring the people to the highest
perfection.
With the Lord granting,
with loving care and most willingly,
I have begotten all things for your
salvation.

Meanwhile I kept giving rewards to
kings,

besides which I kept giving a fee to
their sons,
who walk with me,
and nonetheless they apprehended me
with my companions,
and on that day they wanted most
eagerly to kill me,
but the time had not yet come,
I and all things whatsoever they discovered [lit. "came upon"] with us,
they seized it,
and fettered myself with iron,
and on the fourteenth day the Lord
released me from their power,
and whatsoever was ours was given
back to us on account of God,
and close friends whom we saw to
before.
You furthermore have proved by
experience
how much I have paid out to those

who judged [i.e., the brehons] through
    all the regions
which I kept visiting quite often.
For I reckon that I have distributed
    to them not less than the price of
    fifteen men
so that you might enjoy me,
and I will always enjoy you in God.
It does not cause me regret
nor is it enough to me
that I spend and I shall overspend
    farther.
The Lord is powerful that He may give
    me afterward,
that I may spend myself for your souls.

PART V

Look, I call on God as testifier for my
soul
that I do not lie.
Neither that it be an occasion of
flattery
or of avarice that I shall have written
to you,
nor that I hope for honor from any of
you,
for honor suffices which is not yet seen
but is believed in the heart.

He moreover is faithful Who has
    promised,
He never lies.

But I see now in the present age
myself exalted by the Lord beyond
    measure,
and I was not worthy nor such
that He should supply this to me,
while I know most certainly,
that poverty and calamity has been
    convenient [lit. "come together"],
    better for me
than riches and delights.
But Christ the Lord was also poor for
    us,
for I, pitiable and unhappy,
even if I will have wished, I do not
    now have resources,
nor do I judge myself,
because I hope daily

either massacre or being cheated [lit.
   "gone round"]
or led back into slavery or an occasion
   of some sort.
But I am in awe of none of these things
   on account of the promises of the
   heavens,
because I have hurled myself into the
   hands of all-powerful God,
Who rules as lord everywhere.

Just as the prophet says,
Hurl your thought on God,
and He will nourish you.
Look, now I commend my soul to my
   most faithful God,
for Whom I perform an embassy in my
   ignobility,
but as He does not receive theatrical
   impersonation,
He chose even me for this office,

that I should be one minister from
    among His own least.

Whence moreover shall I hand back to
    Him
for all the things which He has handed
    back to me?
But what shall I say,
or what shall I promise to my Lord,
as I can do nothing
unless Himself will have given to me,
but He examines the hearts and reins,
as enough and too much I want, and I
    was ready
that He should grant to me to drink His
    chalice,
just as He conceded also to others
    loving Him.
On which account it should not befall
    to me from my God
that I should ever lose His own folk

which He has acquired in the furthest
   parts of land.
I pray God that He may give me
   perseverance
and deign that I shall give back to Him
   a faithful testifier
up to the point of my passing over on
   account of my God.
And if I have ever imitated anything of
   the good
on account of my God whom I love
   dearly,
I seek from Him that He give to me
that with those sojourners and captives
   for His own name
I should pour out my blood,
even if I should lack even burial
itself,
or my cadaver be most pitiably divided
   by single members for dogs
or for savage beasts
or birds of heaven should eat it up.

Most certainly I consider,
if this should happen to me,
I have gained the soul as profit with
    my body,
because without any doubt on that day
    we shall rise again in the brightness
    of the sun,
this is, in the glory of Christ Jesus our
    Redeemer,
as sons of the living God and fellow
    heirs of Christ,
and going to be conformed to His
    image,
since from Him and through Him and
    in Him we are going to reign.

For this sun which we see rises daily
    on our account, with Himself order-
    ing it,
but it will never reign, nor will its
    splendor remain forever,
but even all who adore it will come

badly to the punishment of the pitiable.

We moreover who believe and adore the true sun Christ,

Who will never die,

nor he who will have done His will,

but he will remain for eternity,

in the same fashion as Christ also remains for eternity,

Who reigns with God the Father all-powerful,

and with the Holy Spirit before the ages,

and now and through all ages of ages. Amen.

Look, again and again briefly I will set out the words of my Confession.

I bear testimony in truth and in exultation of heart before God and His

holy angels that I have never had
any occasion
besides the Gospel
and His promises
that I should ever go back to that
gentile people
whence earlier I had barely escaped.

But I beseech those believing
and fearing God,
whoever will have deigned to look on
or receive this writing,
which Patrick, a sinner, untaught, to be
sure, wrote down in Ireland,
that no man should ever say that by my
ignorance,
if I have accomplished or demon-
strated any small thing
according to the acceptable purpose of
God,
but that you judge and it must be most
truly believed

that it was the gift of God,
and this is my Confession
before I die.